Visual Geography Series®

POLAND
...in Pictures

Prepared by
Geography Department

Lerner Publications Company
Minneapolis

Independent Picture Service

**A Polish artisan carefully examines the pieces of a violin
before assembling the instrument.**

This book is an all-new edition in the Visual Geography Series. Previous editions were published by
Sterling Publishing Company, New York City. The
text, set in 10/12 Century Textbook, is fully revised
and updated, and new photographs, maps, charts, and
captions have been added.

LIBRARY OF CONGRESS CATALOGING-IN-PUBLICATION DATA

Poland in pictures / prepared by Geography Depart-
   ment, Lerner Publications Company.
   p. cm. — (Visual geography series)
   Includes index.
   Summary: Examines the topography, climate, history,
government, and culture of Poland.
   ISBN 0-8225-1885-6 (lib. bdg.)
   1. Poland. [1. Poland.] I. Lerner Publications Company.
Geography Dept. II. Series: Visual geography series
(Minneapolis, Minn.)
DK4147.P63 1994
943.8—dc20   93-10769
                                            CIP
                                            AC

International Standard Book Number: 0-8225-1885-6
Library of Congress Catalog Card Number: 93-10769

VISUAL GEOGRAPHY SERIES®

Publisher
Harry Jonas Lerner
Senior Editor
Mary M. Rodgers
Editors
Gretchen Bratvold
Tom Streissguth
Colleen Sexton
Photo Researcher
Erica Ackerberg
Editorial/Photo Assistant
Marybeth Campbell
Consultants/Contributors
Carlienne Frisch
Andrzej Jarosznski
Anna Tsarkovich
Sandra K. Davis
Designer
Jim Simondet
Cartographer
Carol F. Barrett
Indexer
Sylvia Timian
Production Manager
Gary J. Hansen

Pronunciation Guide

Bialowieza	bee-ahl-u-VYEZH-eh
Chopin	show-PAN
Czestochowa	chen-steh-HOH-veh
Gdansk	DAHNGSK
Gdynia	DIHNG-yeh
Jagiellonian	yah-geh-LOHN-yian
Kosciuszko	kohs-SHYUS-koh
Lodz	woodzh
Mickiewicz	miks-KEH-vich
Mieszko	mi-EH-shko
Nowa Huta	NOH-vah HOO-ta
Przemysl	PSHEM-ish-shuhl
Sejm	saim
Suchocka	soo-HOTS-kah
Szczecin	SHTET-shin
Walesa	wha-WHEN-sa
Wroclaw	VROWT-slahf

Acknowledgments

Title page photo © Piotrek B. Gorski

Elevation contours adapted from *The Times Atlas of
the World,* seventh comprehensive edition (New York:
Times Books, 1985).

1 2 3 4 5 6 – I/JR – 99 98 97 96 95 94

Residents stroll along the Dlugi Targ ("long market" in the Polish language), a street in the port of Gdansk. Also known as the Royal Road, this route was used by Polish kings to make their entrance into the city.

Contents

BALTIC SEA

LITHUANIA

KALININGRAD
(RUSSIA)

Ustka
Darlowo
Gdynia
Gdansk
Gulf of
Gdansk

Malbork

Tannenberg

Lake
Sniardwy

Szczecin

BELARUS

Warta R.
Poznan
Gniezno
Plock
Bug R.

WARSAW

GERMANY

Nysa

Odra R.

Lodz
Pilica R.

Lublin

Turoszow
Wroclaw
Czestochowa
Czarna R.

Bielawa
Opole

Vistula
San R.

Gliwice Canal
Chorzow
Gliwice
Katowice
Krakow
Nowa Huta
Wieliczka
Oswiecim
(Auschwitz)

Dunajec R.

PIENINY
NAT. PK.

CZECH REPUBLIC

UKRAINE

TATRA
NAT. PK.
Zakopane

POLAND

N

Province Boundaries

Major Roads

0   50   100 Miles
0   50   100 Kilometers

SLOVAKIA

Arctic Circle
NORWEGIAN SEA
20°
0°
20°

EUROPE
POLAND

0   400 Miles
0   400 Kilometers

90°
60°

NORTH
ATLANTIC
OCEAN
20°
40°

MEDITERRANEAN SEA
0°
20°
40°

METRIC CONVERSION CHART
To Find Approximate Equivalents

WHEN YOU KNOW:	MULTIPLY BY:	TO FIND:
AREA		
acres	0.41	hectares
square miles	2.59	square kilometers
CAPACITY		
gallons	3.79	liters
LENGTH		
feet	30.48	centimeters
yards	0.91	meters
miles	1.61	kilometers
MASS (weight)		
pounds	0.45	kilograms
tons	0.91	metric tons
VOLUME		
cubic yards	0.77	cubic meters
TEMPERATURE		
degrees Fahrenheit	0.56 (*after* subtracting 32)	degrees Celsius

Farmers offer food and spices in the city of Lublin. During the 1950s and 1960s, many of Poland's private farmers resisted the seizure of cropland by the Polish Communist government.

Introduction

The Republic of Poland occupies a region of plains, forests, and lakes in north central Europe. *Polska,* which is the country's name in the Polish language, comes from the word *polana,* meaning clearing, or from *pole,* meaning field.

Poland has suffered invasion, conquest, and division, but it has also been the site of great empires. In the sixteenth century, a Polish-led commonwealth stretched across much of central Europe. Internal rivalries weakened this state, and by the late 1700s the Austrian, Prussian, and Russian empires were using their military forces to divide and eliminate Poland. Although their country had ceased to exist, the Poles kept their national culture alive throughout the nineteenth century.

After World War I (1914–1918), the Poles established a new, independent

republic. The country suffered political turmoil and an economic crisis during the 1920s and 1930s. In the summer of 1939, Germany invaded Poland, an action that touched off World War II. Heavy fighting caused widespread death and destruction, and foreign armies again occupied Poland's territory.

As the war ended in 1945, the Soviet Union, a huge Communist state to the east, invaded Poland. Supported by Soviet forces, a Communist government took power, restricted many freedoms, and

This factory in Wroclaw produces electric trams, an important means of public transportation in Polish cities. After World War II (1939–1945), the making of transportation equipment became a large part of Poland's expanding industrial sector.

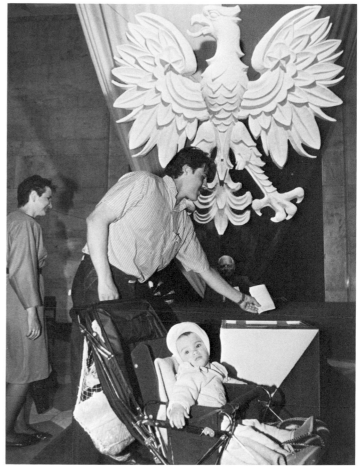

A Polish voter casts his ballot during an election held in June 1989. One of the first open elections in Communist Europe, the vote awarded Solidarity, an independent labor union, a majority of seats in the Polish legislature.

Photo by Polish Information Center

seized ownership of Poland's industry, mining, and agriculture. Poland's Communist leaders jailed many of their opponents and took control of the media. During the next 40 years, government planners set wages, prices, and production levels. But poor economic management eventually caused shortages of food and other consumer goods.

During the 1980s, increasing dissatisfaction with the Communist regime led to a series of strikes organized by Solidarity, an independent labor union. The strikes ignited a widespread revolt against Communism in central Europe and, in 1989, brought about a democratic government in Poland. In the next year, Poles elected Solidarity leader Lech Walesa as their new president. Officials from Solidarity and members of several other non-Communist parties have gained seats in the Polish parliament.

Poland is now going through a difficult period of change and adjustment. The people enjoy the freedom to express their views and to participate in an open political system. At the same time, the country is converting a government-planned economy to a free-market system, in which supply and demand set prices and wages. The free market has caused rising prices, falling production, and unemployment. Despite the hardships, Poles are determined to try this uncertain course in the hope that it will bring a more prosperous future.

The foothills of the Carpathians rise near Zakopane in southern Poland. The area attracts large numbers of tourists who enjoy hiking, camping, and skiing.

1) The Land

Flat plains, river valleys, and gently rolling hills dominate Poland's landscape. A 277-mile coastline on the Baltic Sea forms the country's northern border. In the northeast is Kaliningrad, a part of Russia. To the east are Lithuania, Belarus (formerly Byelorussia), and Ukraine—independent republics that were once part of the Soviet Union. Rugged mountains in the south define boundaries with Slovakia and the Czech Republic. Germany is Poland's western neighbor.

Poland's total land area of 120,727 square miles makes it slightly smaller than the state of New Mexico. From west to east, Poland measures 430 miles. The greatest distance from north to south is 395 miles.

Topography

Poland can be divided into several regions that stretch across the country from west to east. In the north are the Coastal Lowlands, a strip of beaches and lagoons along the shores of the Baltic Sea. Natural harbors exist at Gdansk and Gdynia in the north and at Szczecin in the northwest.

Farther inland, the sparsely populated Lake Region occupies much of northern Poland. Thousands of years ago, glaciers (slow-moving masses of ice) covered the plains of the area. As they retreated northward, the glaciers carved hollows that later became freshwater lakes and peat bogs (swamps filled with decayed plants). The glaciers also formed small, rocky hills known as moraines, which crisscross the land in irregular patterns. Dense forests make lumbering the most important industry in the Lake Region.

The Central Plains, which cover the middle of Poland, are part of the Great European Plain that extends from France in the west to Russia in the east. Moraines and broad river valleys dominate these lowlands, which are intensively farmed. Warsaw, the capital of Poland, straddles the banks of the Vistula River in the

Photo © John R. Kreul

Vines climb along the sides of a narrow lane in the Polish countryside.

Photo by George S. Thomson

A crowded raft floats downstream through Poland's southern mountains.

eastern part of the Central Plains. The Bialowieza Forest—one of the largest in Europe—lies northeast of Warsaw on the Belarussian border.

The rolling hills of the Polish Uplands reach about 1,000 feet in elevation south of the Central Plains. In the southwest, the region of Silesia, which extends into the Czech Republic and Germany, contains important industrial centers and most of Poland's mineral resources. The plateaus and hills of this area also support farms.

The Carpathian Forelands cover a long, narrow territory between the Vistula and the San rivers in southeastern Poland. Rich soil supports a wide variety of crops in this region. In the southwest, the Sudeten Mountains rise to 5,000 feet above sea level. Forests cover the rounded peaks of these highlands, which are separated from the Carpathian Mountains to the east by a pass called the Moravian Gate.

The Beskid and Tatra ranges, spurs of the Carpathians, line Poland's southern border. Rysy Peak, the highest point in Poland, towers 8,199 feet in the Tatras. In these mountains live the *Gorale* people, who speak their own dialect of Polish and who have maintained many of their traditional customs.

Rivers and Lakes

For centuries, navigable rivers and canals have provided Poland with an important shipping network. This system also links Poland with foreign countries through seaports on the Baltic coast.

Sheep graze in a meadow high in the Tatra Mountains, a range that extends along Poland's border with Slovakia.

The Old Town of Gdansk faces a waterway near the city's harbor. An ancient port and trading center, Gdansk was founded more than 1,000 years ago. Although more than 90 percent of the city was destroyed during World War II, the people of Gdansk rebuilt their historic homes and churches after the conflict.

Poland's longest river, the Vistula, begins in the Tatra Mountains. Navigable over much of its course, the Vistula flows 670 miles northward through central Poland before emptying into the Gulf of Gdansk. The Bug River, a tributary of the Vistula, forms part of Poland's boundary with Ukraine and Belarus. Several other rivers flow westward into the Vistula from outside Poland's borders.

The Odra and the Nysa rivers follow Poland's western boundary with Germany. The Odra begins in the mountains of Slovakia, flows northwest, and ends at a wide lagoon on the Baltic Sea north of Szczecin. Feeding the Odra are the Warta River and several small streams in central and western Poland.

Rivers, streams, and canals connect thousands of lakes in the plains and forests of Poland's Lake Region. The Masurian Lakes in the northeast and the Pomeranian Lakes in the northwest are popular spots for camping, fishing, and water sports. Lake Sniardwy, the country's largest lake, covers 36 square miles.

A guide steers his raft down the Dunajec River in Pieniny National Park. The Dunajec rafts are made of dugout canoes fastened together by sturdy ropes. Tourists have enjoyed rafting on the rapids of the Dunajec since the nineteenth century.

Smaller lakes exist in Poland's mountainous regions, where glaciers carved shallow basins between the steep slopes.

Climate

Poland's weather varies greatly, depending on each region's elevation and distance from the seacoast. Mild ocean winds bring cool summers and moderate winters to the Baltic shore, where temperatures average 31° F in January, the coldest month, and 63° F in July, the warmest month. Warm sea currents allow the harbor of Gdansk to remain ice-free all year.

Interior regions of Poland have slightly colder winters and warmer summers. In Warsaw, the average temperature is 27° F in January and 67° F in July. Temperatures are lowest in the mountains of the south, which have the country's highest elevations. The *halny,* a dry wind, occa-

Children feed a group of swans in Warsaw's Lazienki Park.

sionally blows from the south, moderating the cold temperatures of this area.

Frequent showers and thunderstorms interrupt Poland's dry, cool summer days. Annual precipitation averages 24 inches on the plains, while certain areas of the Carpathian Mountains receive 60 or more inches of rain and snow a year. Snow covers the Carpathians for one to three months during the winter.

Flora and Fauna

Industrial pollution and natural diseases have damaged many of Poland's forests, which now cover about one-fourth of the country's land. The Bialowieza Forest, the only untouched forest in central Europe, lies 160 miles east of Warsaw. Stands of yew and mountain ash trees flourish in the Tuchola Forest, which stretches from the Vistula River westward to the lakes of north central Poland.

Large tracts of timber in the north and in the Carpathian Mountains supply Poland's lumber industry. About 75 per-

cent of these trees are evergreens, such as pine, spruce, and fir. Deciduous (leaf-shedding) trees—including ash, poplar, willow, birch, beech, elm, oak, and alder—are common in the Lake Region, in the Central Plains, and in the south.

Poland's national parks shelter a wide variety of uncommon plants. Visitors to Tatra National Park can see rare stone pine and edelweiss, a small herb that grows at high elevations. Cheddar pink and tormentil grow in the forests of the Lake Region, and the martagon lily thrives in the southern mountains.

Although Poles have cleared vast tracts of forested land and destroyed much natural habitat, wildlife has survived in several regions. The Bialowieza Forest is home to bison, elks, lynxes, bears, tarpans (wild ponies), and foxes. Wild boars, wolves, and mountain deer roam the valleys and forests of the Carpathian Mountains. The Polish government officially protects the wild swans, cormorants, and black storks that inhabit the lakes and rivers of the north.

13

The lignite (soft coal) mine at Turoszow is one of the largest coal mines in Poland. The smokestacks and cooling towers of a massive, coal-fired power station rise in the distance.

In the 1950s, engineers discovered vast copper deposits in western Poland. Copper and coal have since become the country's main mineral exports. Workers also mine deposits of sulfur, iron ore, lead, and zinc.

Rock salt deposits in southern and central Poland, estimated at 11 billion tons, are among the world's largest. A gigantic mine at Wieliczka, near Krakow, has produced salt for many centuries. Deposits of amber (fossilized tree resin)—a material used in jewelry making—exist on the Baltic seacoast. Poland taps small fields of oil and natural gas in the foothills of the Carpathian Mountains.

Cities

World War II drastically affected the people and the cities of Poland. Wartime losses, emigration, and forced resettlement

Despite severe river and coastal pollution from cities and industries, nearly 50 species of fish have survived in Poland. The most common are pike, trout, salmon, miller's-thumb, whitefish, eel, and crayfish. Commercial fishers harvest herring and cod from the Baltic Sea.

Natural Resources

Silesia and the Polish Uplands contain most of the country's mineral wealth. Poland's chief natural resource is coal, an essential fuel for energy production and industry. Reserves of 40 billion tons of lignite (soft coal) exist in southwestern and central Poland. One of the world's largest coal fields lies near the southern city of Katowice.

Long Street extends through Stare Miasto (Old Town), the historic center of Warsaw.

reduced the country's population by about one-third. After the war, many farmers abandoned their rural villages and sought jobs in Poland's cities, where a rapid program of rebuilding and industrialization created new homes and jobs.

About 60 percent of Poland's 38.5 million people now live in cities. Many large urban centers lie within a vast industrial and mining zone in the Polish Uplands. Smaller towns and cities dot the Central Plains, while the Baltic coast region includes several major ports.

WARSAW

Warsaw grew along the banks of the Vistula River in east central Poland. Home to 1.7 million people, the city has been a trading hub since the fifteenth century and the capital of Poland since 1596. Warsaw experienced war and occupation in the

A statue of King Sigismund III Vasa dominates Warsaw's Castle Square. The column, a famous symbol of the capital, was the first monument in Warsaw to be restored after World War II. Behind it stands a section of the fifteenth-century wall that once surrounded the city.

The Ratusz (City Hall) in Poznan dates from the 1500s, a time of great power and prosperity for this Polish city.

15

Restored homes line a square in Warsaw's Old Town. By carefully following old drawings, photographs, and building plans, architects reconstructed every structure in Old Town, which had been leveled by bombing and street fighting during World War II.

eighteenth and nineteenth centuries, as stronger European states fought over Polish territory.

During World War II, aerial bombing and street fighting destroyed 90 percent of the buildings in Warsaw, and the city's population fell from more than one million to 160,000. The Poles later used old photos and drawings as a guide to rebuild Stare Miasto (Old Town), the capital's ancient center. Engineers and architects reconstructed houses, palaces, churches, and a royal castle. Contrasting sharply with Stare Miasto are the modern stores, offices, and high-rise apartments of the downtown Centrum complex. The Palace of Culture and Science, a skyscraper built under Poland's Communist regime, towers over the city.

An important transportation hub, Warsaw is also an industrial center that produces steel, cars, chemicals, textiles, and

A modern skyscraper rises near a busy street in Warsaw. The fall of Europe's Communist regimes—as well as more open trade between eastern and western Europe—has made Warsaw an important financial center.

beer. Students attend several major universities in the city, a lively cultural center that boasts museums, libraries, theaters, and concert halls.

SECONDARY CITIES

Poland's oldest city, Krakow (population 743,700) lies along the Vistula about 150 miles south of Warsaw. Founded around A.D. 700, Krakow later became a commercial and political center. It was Poland's capital city from the early fourteenth century until 1596. Jagiellonian University, the country's oldest university, was founded in Krakow in 1364.

Poland's kings were crowned in Krakow's fourteenth-century cathedral, which contains the tombs of many famous Poles. Market Square, lined by palaces and old mansions, is a traditional setting for festivals and national celebrations. The

German army made the city its occupation headquarters during World War II and spared many of Krakow's ancient buildings and homes from destruction.

Modern Krakow is a trading center for minerals, agricultural products, and timber. The massive iron and steel works at nearby Nowa Huta make the surrounding region one of Poland's principal manufacturing areas. Factories within Krakow furnish building materials, machinery, and chemicals.

The city of Lodz (population 851,500), in central Poland, has thrived from textile production for more than a century. Under Russian control from 1815 to 1918, Lodz supplied cotton and woolen cloth to Russia and the Soviet Union until after World War II. Hundreds of textile mills still operate alongside chemical and metallurgical factories. Poland's Communist

Pigeons flock to Krakow's vast Market Square. Cafes and flower stalls line the square, which was designed in the fourteenth century.

17

Students march in a masked parade in Gdansk. Youth festivals—also known as Juvenalia—take place every year in Polish university towns. One of the highlights of these annual events is a boisterous masquerade.

government moved some industry out of the city in the 1950s to lower its high population density.

Wroclaw (population 637,000) lies on the Odra River about 200 miles southwest of Warsaw. A railroad and industrial center, Wroclaw was for centuries the capital of the German-speaking region of Lower Silesia. A hub of Poland's electronics and computer industries, Wroclaw is also a leading producer of railcars. A network of canals and tributaries crosses Wroclaw and its surrounding region, and Poles have nicknamed Wroclaw "the city of bridges."

Poland's major seaports, including Gdynia, Gdansk, and Szczecin, rise near natural lagoons and gulfs on the Baltic coast. Gdansk (population 461,000), on the Gulf of Gdansk, began as a fishing village in the late 900s and has been a major port since the 1500s. In 1980 workers in the Gdansk shipyards formed the Solidarity union, the first independent labor organization in any Communist nation.

Scaffolding surrounds a freighter under construction in the shipyards of Gdynia. Until the 1920s, Gdynia was a small fishing village. After the nation achieved independence, the port expanded rapidly. By 1939 it had become one of the largest ports on the Baltic Sea.

Built by King Sigismund I, the Royal Castle in Krakow was the seat of power for Poland's kings until the capital was moved to Warsaw in 1596.

2) History and Government

Archaeologists believe that humans have lived in Poland for at least 200,000 years, but very little is known about the region's earliest inhabitants. Prehistoric peoples first formed communities in Poland's river valleys about 15,000 years ago. In the first century A.D., ethnic Slavs from the east moved into the lowlands of central and northern Poland.

The Polanie (plain dwellers), a Slavic group, built small towns called *grody* in the region of the Warta River. Because Poland's lowlands and plains offered little protection from attack, the Polanie constructed strong wooden walls around their settlements. Outside the walls, the Polanie cleared land to raise grain and livestock. The people of the grody traded their goods and handicrafts with other Slavic groups inhabiting central Europe.

For several centuries, the Slavs remained untouched by events in western Europe. Armies of the Roman Empire, which was based in southern Europe, had conquered a vast realm by A.D. 100. Although a road linked Poland's Baltic coast with Roman towns to the south, the empire never subdued Slavic peoples in eastern Europe. Nor did early Roman Catholic missionaries, who spread the Christian faith to Germany, succeed in gaining converts among the Polanie.

As the population of Poland increased, the Slavic peoples divided into groups, some of which migrated from the area. Between A.D. 200 and A.D. 500, the Eastern Slavs moved to the areas that would become Belarus, Ukraine, and Russia. The Western Slavs, a group that included the Polanie, inhabited the territory of Poland as well as the future lands of the Czechs and the Slovaks to the south.

The Piast Dynasty

The Polanie, who inhabited about 20 independent communities, built new towns in the basins of the Vistula and Odra rivers. Large, organized Polanie states arose in the south near Krakow and in the west near Poznan. Trading centers also developed along the Baltic seacoast. The Polanie built fortified castles to protect their land from the attacks of German Catholic crusaders (religious warriors), who sought to convert the Slavic peoples to Christianity by force.

To resist these invasions, the Polanie united in the mid-ninth century under Piast, a ruler celebrated in Polish tales and legends. By the tenth century, the members of the Piast dynasty (family of rulers) were bringing the people of the plains, the Lake Region, and the Baltic coast under their control. In 966 Prince Mieszko I established the capital of the Piast state at Gniezno, near Poznan.

To strengthen his realm's defenses and to stop the attacks of German crusaders, Mieszko allied with the Holy Roman Empire, a confederation of states in central Europe. Prince Mieszko also formed an alliance with Bohemia, a Slavic state to the south, by marrying a Bohemian princess. Mieszko converted to Roman Catholicism, the faith of his new wife, and invited Catholic missionaries to Poland. In 1025 the pope—the Catholic church leader—officially recognized the Polish realm by crowning Boleslaus I, Mieszko's son and successor. The Poles adopted the Latin alphabet, which was used by the Roman Catholic Church, to write their Slavic language.

In the tenth century, Prince Mieszko I married Dubravka, a Roman Catholic from Bohemia, and welcomed Catholic missionaries to Poland. As a result, Mieszko brought about his nation's conversion to the Christian faith and ended attacks from the west by armies of German Catholic crusaders (religious warriors).

Photo by Polish Information Center

The Royal Castle rises on Wawel Hill in the city of Krakow, which became the capital of Poland under King Boleslaus III. Even after the royal court and government were moved to Warsaw, the castle remained the burial place of Polish monarchs, poets, and patriots.

A brave and ambitious ruler, King Boleslaus conquered land in Germany and extended his realm as far east as the Dnieper River, which flows southward through Ukraine and empties into the Black Sea. Trade along the Dnieper linked Poland with Black Sea ports and helped the Polish kingdom to prosper.

At the same time, a dispute among church leaders was dividing Christianity into two factions. This led to the founding of the Eastern Orthodox Church in the eleventh century. Orthodox Christianity was centered in the city of Constantinople (modern Istanbul, Turkey). Although many of the eastern European Slavs became Orthodox Christians, the people of Poland and Bohemia were allied with the pope and remained within the Roman Catholic Church.

Decline and Invasion

Poland experienced violent internal conflicts after the death of Boleslaus I in 1025. When Boleslaus II disputed with the Polish nobility, the Catholic bishop of Krakow took the side of the nobles. In 1079 Boleslaus ordered the murder of the bishop, an action that led the pope to impose sanctions (penalties) on Poland.

The Poles were also fighting with their German neighbors. In the early 1100s,

Photo by Polish Information Center

Boleslaus I was the first Polish ruler to be officially recognized by the pope, the leader of the powerful Roman Catholic Church.

21

Opole, the ancient capital of an independent Polish principality, was seized by Bohemia in 1327. In the eighteenth century, Prussia annexed (took over) the city during the partition of Poland. Opole remained part of Germany until the end of World War II, when a treaty returned Opole and the surrounding province to Poland.

Independent Picture Service

Boleslaus III battled the forces of the Holy Roman Empire for control of Pomerania (northwestern Poland). But he weakened Poland by decreeing that his kingdom would be divided equally among his sons. During the next two centuries, this system of inheritance created many small, semi-independent principalities (realms of princes). Rivalries among the Polish nobles and princes left the Polish people disorganized and powerless to defend their long frontiers.

Poland's neighbors quickly took advantage of the growing chaos within the kingdom. The Order of Teutonic Knights, an organization of Catholic warriors, attacked from the north. Lithuania, a nation on the Baltic Sea to the northeast, also invaded Polish lands. In 1240 a huge force of Mongolian Tatars advanced from their base in eastern Asia to devastate Poland and much of eastern Europe.

After the Tatars retreated from Europe, Poland began a slow recovery. German artisans and merchants were invited to settle in Polish towns and ports. Poland also welcomed large numbers of Jews who were fleeing persecution in other European nations. Membership in the Hanseatic League—a commercial union of northern European cities—allowed trade to flourish in Krakow, Gdansk, and other cities of the kingdom.

CASIMIR THE GREAT

After the assassination of the Polish king Przemysl II in 1295, a dispute erupted over the succession to the throne. The king of Bohemia, Wenceslas II, sought to extend his power in the region by attacking Polish territory. After the death of Wenceslas in 1305, a member of the Piast dynasty gained support from the pope and was crowned King Ladislas I in 1320. Following his coronation in Krakow, Ladislas made the city the new Polish capital.

Poland was still a weak and divided nation when Ladislas's son Casimir III, or Casimir the Great, began ruling in 1333. By strengthening the monarchy's control over Poland, Casimir ended internal conflicts and reunified the nation. He also secured Poland's borders by forming alliances with Lithuania and with Hungary, a powerful kingdom to the south.

Casimir made many important internal reforms. He established laws to protect the rights of the Polish peasants (rural farm laborers). The king also reorganized Poland's laws and administration. A patron of education, Casimir founded the nation's first university at Krakow in 1364.

The Jagiellonian Dynasty

After Casimir died in 1370 without an heir, his nephew King Louis of Hungary took the throne. Jadwiga, the daughter of Louis, became Poland's queen in 1382. Four years later, Jadwiga married the Lithuanian duke Jogaila. The Polish nobles, who sought Lithuania's help in battling the Teutonic Knights, elected Jogaila as King Wladislaw II Jagiello in 1386. Although Poland and Lithuania still had separate governments, the two nations were now ruled by the Jagiellonian dynasty.

The Jagiellonian rulers scored several decisive military victories during the fifteenth century. In 1410 an army of Poles and Lithuanians defeated the Teutonic Knights at the Battle of Tannenberg. After losing several more battles to Wladislaw's successor, Casimir IV, the Teutonic Knights agreed to the Peace of Thorn and gave up lands in Prussia (northeastern Germany) to Poland.

In 1410 a combined army of Lithuanians and Poles defeated the Teutonic Knights at the Battle of Tannenberg. The battle ended the Knights' challenge to the Jagiellonian dynasty, which ruled Polish and Lithuanian lands in north central Europe.

A building of the Jagiellonian University, Poland's oldest institution of higher learning, surrounds a courtyard. The astronomer Mikolaj Kopernik, also known as Copernicus, began studying here at the age of 18. A historical museum at the university now displays the famous Jagiellonian Globe, the first to show the Western Hemisphere.

A stamp commemorates the 500th anniversary of the birth of Copernicus, who challenged the popular notion that the earth was the center of the solar system.

After the signing of the Peace of Thorn, Poland reached the height of its power and influence in central Europe. Under Jagiellonian rule, the kingdom also made important economic, political, and cultural advances. Printers produced the first Polish books around 1520. Poland's scholars founded new universities and began to use Polish instead of Latin, the traditional language of religion and scholarship in Europe. The Polish astronomer Mikolaj Kopernik, also known by his Latin name Copernicus, made important discoveries that laid the foundation for modern astronomy.

While these changes were in progress, however, the Christian faith was in turmoil. A revolt against the Catholic church erupted in Germany, where the teachings of Martin Luther sparked the Protestant Reformation. Protestant churches—which did not recognize the authority of the Catholic pope—were founded in several northern European countries, including the Scandinavian kingdom of Sweden. Although it remained a Catholic nation, Poland allowed members of other faiths to worship freely. Poland became a center of Jewish culture, and its Jewish community became one of the largest in the world.

THE POLISH PARLIAMENT

During the reign of Casimir IV, a class of warriors and landowners called the *szlachta* increased its control over Poland's land and peasant farmers. High taxes on the peasants forced many of them to become serfs—rural workers who were bound to the estates of the landowners.

The growing power of the upper classes had allowed them to form a national parliament in 1493. This legislature included a senate of wealthy nobles and a Sejm, or lower house, of landowners. In 1505 the parliament wrote the nation's first constitution, which stated that the Polish kings could pass no new laws without the parliament's consent. The Sejm also gave itself the power to vote approval of each king.

In 1569, shortly before the end of the Jagiellonian dynasty, Poland and Lithuania formally united under Polish authority. After the unification, Poland's kings ruled a huge realm that included Germans, Poles, Lithuanians, and Ukrainians. Sigismund II, the last Jagiellonian ruler, died in 1572.

FOREIGN PRINCES RULE POLAND

After Sigismund's death, the Polish nobles increased their power by assuming the right to elect future kings. This led to intense rivalries within Poland, which the parliament tried to calm by electing foreign princes to the Polish throne. In 1575 the parliament elected as king Stephen Bathory, a Hungarian prince. A strong military leader, Bathory defeated an invasion of Poland ordered by Ivan IV, the czar (emperor) of Russia.

Sigismund III Vasa, a Swedish prince, succeeded Bathory in 1586. Vasa was the first of several Swedes to become kings of Poland. But this arrangement eventually caused a religious war between Protestant Sweden and Catholic Poland. Swedish

King Alexander I presides over the Crown Council, a body of advisers that later developed into the Polish parliament. By the end of the 1500s, the parliament's nobles had the power to elect Poland's monarchs.

forces invaded Poland in 1655, burning and pillaging towns and farms.

The Poles stopped this invasion, but many years of military conflict and economic decline followed. The Cossacks, a group of free peasants who lived in areas of Ukraine and Russia, had seized Polish territory before the Swedish invasion. Fierce and capable soldiers, the Cossacks recognized no outside authority. They brought into their ranks many Ukrainian peasants opposed to Polish rule. As Polish authority weakened, the growing Russian Empire was able to seize large sections of eastern Poland.

Another threat came from the Ottoman Turks, who had conquered Constantinople and much of eastern Europe from their base in Asia Minor (modern Turkey). In 1683 Jan Sobieski—who had been elected King John III of Poland in 1674—defeated the Turks at Vienna, Austria. His victory stopped the Turkish advance into central Europe.

The Partitions of Poland

Despite Sobieski's triumph, conflict within the Polish parliament shook the kingdom. Under King Augustus II, a German who had succeeded Jan Sobieski, Poland began to lose its independence to its stronger neighbors. When Augustus died in 1733, Russia was able to block the accession of a Polish noble. Instead, the representatives of the Russian czar bribed a large faction of the Sejm to elect Augustus's son.

At the same time, heavy taxes were causing a drop in Polish agriculture and trade. Poland's military declined, leaving the kingdom defenseless against foreign armies. The nobility did little to unite Poland's rival political factions and weakened the realm through their incom-

To avoid feuding among Poland's nobles, the Sejm often elected foreigners to rule the nation. But Jan Sobieski, who was elected king in 1674, was a Polish-born military hero. By defeating the Turks at Vienna in 1683, Sobieski stopped the advance of the Ottoman Empire into central Europe.

Courtesy of Library of Congress

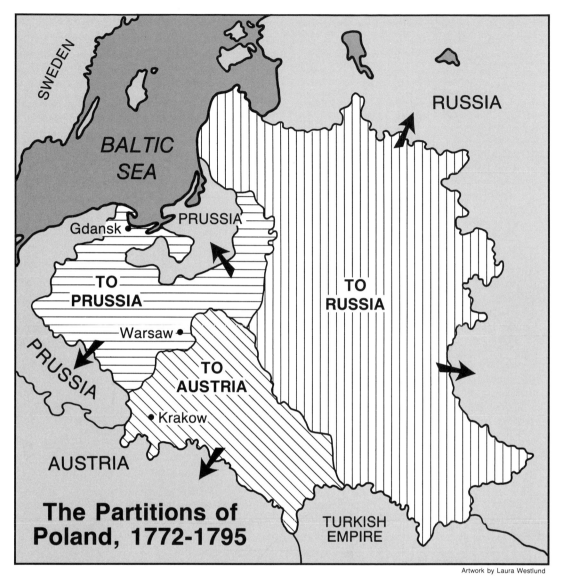

The Partitions of Poland, 1772-1795

The partitions of Polish territory by Austria, Prussia, and Russia ended Poland's existence as an independent nation.

petence and corruption. In addition, the Sejm had adopted the Liberum Veto. Under this system, a single member of parliament had the power to stop new laws from being passed.

The Liberum Veto led to governmental chaos, which gave Poland's enemies an opportunity to capture Polish territory. In 1772 Prussia and Austria—two strong realms to the west and south, respectively—joined with Russia in annexing

(seizing) nearly one-third of Poland's land. This was the first of three partitions of Poland.

In the years following the first partition, a movement for governmental reform gathered force in the Polish parliament. Despite the opposition of many Polish nobles, the legislature adopted a new constitution in 1791. This document reduced the Sejm's power by abolishing the Liberum Veto and by making the crown

During the 1770s, Tadeusz Kosciuszko joined the armies of the North American colonists in their war for independence from Britain. After returning to Europe, however, Kosciuszko was unsuccessful in fighting against the Russian occupation of Poland.

hereditary instead of elective. The new constitution also guaranteed the legal rights of all citizens.

The Russian czarina (empress), Catherine II, did not want her own citizens demanding such reforms, however. With the cooperation of several Polish nobles, she ordered the invasion and seizure of eastern Poland. At the same time, the Prussians took some western land and the port of Gdansk.

This second partition of Poland inspired a revolt led by the Polish patriot Tadeusz Kosciuszko. In 1794 Kosciuszko defeated a Russian army at Warsaw, but the combined forces of Russia and Prussia outnumbered the Poles. In the following year, Russia, Prussia, and Austria crushed Kosciuszko's revolt and forced the Polish king to abdicate. The three empires divided the remaining Polish territory among themselves, and the kingdom of Poland ceased to exist.

Foreign Rule and World War I

Following the third partition, many Polish soldiers and politicians emigrated to France, where a popular revolution had toppled the French monarchy. Polish military leaders formed fighting units in France in the hope of one day liberating their nation. Under the French general Napoleon Bonaparte, these units fought with the French army against Austria and Prussia. After defeating Prussia in 1807, Napoleon established the Grand Duchy of Warsaw, a democratic state under French administration.

A coalition of several nations defeated Napoleon in 1815 and founded a small kingdom of Poland under Russian control. Polish lands annexed by the Grand Duchy were returned to Prussia and Austria. During the reign of the Russian czar Alexander I, the kingdom of Poland gained a new constitution and made important advances in industry and education.

Yet the Polish people demanded complete independence. When a rebellion broke out in 1830, the czar reacted by incorporating eastern Poland into the Russian Empire. Russia abolished the Polish constitution and parliament and seized control of Poland's economy. By the 1860s, Russian had become the language of administration and education in what had once been Poland.

Foreign rule in western Poland was even more strict. In the 1870s, the Prussian chancellor Otto von Bismarck, who united several German-speaking states into the German Empire, tried to eliminate Polish culture in the lands under his control. The German government closed Polish Catholic schools, restricted the activities of the Catholic church, and forced Poles in Pomerania and Silesia to use the German language. Western Poland benefited, however, from Germany's own industrial development, which included the construction of a modern railroad system.

Although they had lost their independence, Poles struggled to keep their na-

Artwork by Laura Westlund

The white eagle and red shield have been Polish national symbols since the 1200s, and their colors are still used in the Polish flag. Poland adopted the current design of its flag upon gaining independence after World War I (1914–1918).

tional identity. Violent uprisings against Russian rule inspired sympathy among many European leaders and helped Polish patriotism to remain strong. Polish writers, artists, and musicians glorified their vanished nation and kept their culture alive by drawing on Polish folk traditions.

By the early twentieth century, the nations of Europe had formed two strong alliances to balance the continent's rival powers. Britain sided with France and Russia to oppose Germany, Austria, and the Ottoman Empire. The Poles joined new political parties that sought the

Born in Warsaw, the scientist Marie Curie-Sklodowska spent much of her life in Paris. Working with her husband, Pierre, she discovered the elements of polonium (named for her homeland of Poland) and radium. In 1903 she became the first woman to receive a Nobel Prize.

Courtesy of Consulate of Poland

A procession marches through the streets of Warsaw to celebrate Polish independence in 1918.

Photo by Polish Information Center

support of the European powers. Under the politician Roman Dmowski, the National Democratic party formed ties with Russia. The Polish Socialist party and its leader Jozef Pilsudski allied with Austria.

In the summer of 1914, World War I broke out between the two European alliances. Poland became a battleground for the armies of Austria, Germany, and Russia. A series of defeats eventually forced the Russians to sign a peace treaty with Germany in March 1918. Later that year, however, Germany and Austria surrendered and World War I came to an end.

The Republic of Poland

During the war, revolutionaries known as Communists had overthrown the Russian government. After withdrawing from World War I, the Russian Communist regime recognized the right of the Poles to choose their own form of government. As the war ended, a provisional (temporary) Polish government founded the independent Republic of Poland. Jozef Pilsudski, a military hero, became Poland's chief of state.

The postwar Treaty of Versailles disarmed Germany and set new borders in northern and central Europe. The pact granted Poland territory from Germany as well as a strip of land along the Vistula River as far as the Baltic Sea coast. Gdansk, whose population was mostly German-speaking, became the free city of Danzig. The treaty placed the city under the administration of an international association known as the League of Nations.

Pilsudski's goal was to reestablish the frontiers of Poland that existed before the partitions. This policy brought Poland into conflict with Russia, where Communists were fighting the supporters of czarist rule. In 1920 Russia and Poland skirmished along their border. Taking advantage of the chaos within Russia, the Poles seized land beyond their eastern frontier. In 1921 Poland and Russia finally signed a peace treaty.

The Russian Communists eventually defeated their czarist opponents and, in 1922, founded the Union of Soviet Socialist Republics (USSR). In the same year, Poland's legislature drafted a new constitution, and Pilsudski resigned as Poland's chief of state.

During the 1920s, the reestablished Sejm passed reforms in education, labor laws, and landownership. Industrial workers formed trade unions, and peasants in the countryside gained private land for raising crops. To help Polish trade, the government built a new port on the Baltic Sea at Gdynia.

Although Polish leaders were successfully rebuilding Poland, competing political factions weakened the government. In addition, opposition to Polish rule by ethnic Ukrainians, Germans, and Belarussians, as well as rising prices and widespread unemployment, caused a political crisis. By 1926 the ongoing problems had paralyzed the government.

Many Poles considered Marshal Jozef Pilsudski a national hero. But when conflict divided Poland's government in the mid-1920s, Pilsudski used the backing of the military to seize dictatorial powers.

Disappointed by the failures of Poland's legislature—and backed by the military—Pilsudski returned in 1926 and overthrew the Polish government. He limited the powers of the Sejm and appointed a close ally as prime minister. During the late 1920s and early 1930s, Pilsudski commanded the armed forces and ruled Poland as a dictator.

New threats to Polish security arose during the 1930s. In Germany the Nazi regime of Adolf Hitler came to power and quickly began to rearm. In 1938 Hitler seized part of Czechoslovakia, which had been established south of Poland after World War I. Hitler also demanded the return of Danzig to German control.

To the east, the Soviet leader Joseph Stalin claimed eastern Poland as Soviet territory. In the summer of 1939, Hitler and Stalin signed a secret agreement to invade and divide Poland. As Poland rejected Hitler's demands, Britain and France pledged to help Poland in the event of a German attack.

World War II

On September 1, 1939, German armies staged a massive invasion of Poland. At the same time, the forces of the Soviet Union attacked from the east. Within two days, Britain and France declared war on Germany, but they were unable to stop

Artwork by Laura Westlund

The German attack on Poland in September 1939 touched off World War II, a global conflict fought between Allied and Axis nations. Located between the Soviet Union and Germany, Poland became a center of the fighting in 1944, when Soviet forces drove into central Europe.

Photo by Nelson Helm

A wire fence surrounds the concentration camp at Oswiecim (Auschwitz), which the occupying German forces built during World War II. At Auschwitz and other camps, the Germans executed millions of Jews, Gypsies, and political opponents. After the war, the Polish government restored and preserved Auschwitz as a memorial.

German and Soviet forces from over-running Poland. As Warsaw fell, Polish politicians escaped to Britain to form a government-in-exile.

The German occupation of Polish cities caused massive damage. Bombing and ground fighting destroyed Danzig, Warsaw, and several other industrial centers. As World War II continued, the Nazis built concentration camps in Poland where millions of political prisoners and ethnic minorities were put to death. More than three million Polish Jews lost their lives during the war.

After Hitler attacked the Soviet Union in 1941, German armies occupied all of Poland. By 1944, however, a Soviet counterattack was forcing the Germans to retreat. The Soviets soon occupied Poland, and with Soviet forces driving on the German capital of Berlin, the Nazi government finally surrendered in May 1945.

Courtesy of National Archives

A column of German soldiers drives through a ruined Polish city during World War II. The occupation of Poland by Germany and the Soviet Union resulted in widespread death and destruction.

Mounds of rubble line the streets of Warsaw in 1945. Street fighting during the war destroyed 90 percent of the city, which also lost most of its population.

During the war, the United States and Britain recognized the members of the Polish government-in-exile as the official leaders of Poland. After the war, however, the exiles were challenged by the Committee of National Liberation, an organization dominated by Polish Communists. With his army occupying Poland, Stalin was able to force the election of Communists to important government posts. Unable to challenge Stalin or the Committee of National Liberation, the leaders of the government-in-exile did not return home.

Poland under Communism

The USSR, Britain, and the United States agreed on Poland's new boundaries in 1945. The Soviet Union annexed 70,000 square miles from Poland's eastern area, and 40,000 square miles of German territory were added to western Poland. The border changes forced eight million Germans to flee northern and western Poland.

After the war, the Polish Communists organized the Polish United Workers' party, a group modeled on the Communist party of the Soviet Union. The United Workers' party founded trade unions and set up committees to administer cities and provinces. In 1947 the party fixed elections to bring about a Communist majority in the Polish parliament. Communist leaders later renamed their country the People's Republic of Poland.

The Polish government eventually put all private businesses under state control. Government planners set prices for goods and wages for workers. Farmers were forced to join agricultural collectives, on which the planting, harvesting, and sale of crops were under state direction. The government seized church lands, arrested critics of the regime, and forced opposition parties to reorganize under Communist control.

Poland became part of a Communist bloc of nations in central Europe, in which trade and industry were closely tied to the Soviet economy. The Polish government, for example, built new factories to produce heavy machinery and other industrial goods for export to the Soviet Union. The leaders of the Soviet regime exercised control over Poland's economy and political life, and Polish Communists who objected to Soviet influence lost their positions. In 1948 the government imprisoned Wladyslaw Gomulka, a Polish Communist leader, for publicly disagreeing with Soviet policy.

Polish students, artists, and workers still resisted the regime, and in 1956 violent antigovernment riots broke out in Poznan. In response, the Polish government released Gomulka, who became the first secretary (head) of the Polish Communist party.

Gomulka freed imprisoned Catholic clergy, returned most collectivized land to private farmers, and increased contact with western Europe. Throughout the 1960s, however, Gomulka followed most of the policies set by the Soviet leadership. Opposition to Communism continued within Poland, and, after widespread rioting erupted in 1970 over poor economic conditions, the party forced Gomulka to resign.

A huge iron foundry rises in Nowa Huta, a manufacturing center near Krakow. Located near the extensive coal fields of Silesia, Nowa Huta became a major hub of Poland's postwar industrialization.

Courtesy of Robert Obojski

A stamp illustrates a visit to Auschwitz by Pope John Paul II. As the first Polish pope in history, John Paul used his authority and popularity to encourage Polish democracy during the 1980s.

of Solidarity, a national labor union headed by Lech Walesa, a shipyard electrician and strike organizer.

The rights gained by Polish workers put pressure on the government to enact other reforms. Gierek released political prisoners and lessened central control over the country's newspapers and other media. But the Soviet and Polish Communist leaders opposed these changes. The Poles feared

The new premier, Edward Gierek, planned to further Poland's industrialization with huge loans from western European nations. Despite his efforts, the country's economy continued to decline. Poor harvests affected the supply of food, and in 1976 the government tried to balance its budget by increasing food prices. Violent street demonstrations quickly forced the regime to back down.

The Solidarity Movement

By 1980 the Poles were suffering serious shortages of food, consumer goods, and electrical power. In the summer, workers at the Lenin Shipyard in Gdansk protested conditions by walking off the job. Workers in other Polish cities followed, and the three-week strike paralyzed the country. The government eventually agreed to most of the workers' demands, including wage increases and the right to organize unions independent of Communist control. The successful strike led to the founding

Courtesy of Consulate of Poland

President Lech Walesa observes a ceremony at the Royal Castle in Krakow. A shipyard electrician from Gdansk, Walesa led strikes by the port's workers as the head of the Solidarity movement. In 1990, after the fall of the Communist government, Poles elected him to the new post of president.

In June 1993, Prime Minister Hanna Suchocka suffered a vote of "no confidence" by the legislature, whose members indicated they no longer favored her policies. New elections in September brought the Democratic Left Alliance and the Polish Peasants party a majority in the parliament. This coalition, which favors slowing the pace of economic reform, replaced Suchocka with Waldemar Pawlak.

Courtesy of Republic of Poland Government Press Office

military intervention or an overthrow of their government by the Soviet Union. In 1981 Gierek resigned and was replaced by Wojciech Jaruzelski, a strict Communist.

Jaruzelski outlawed Solidarity and ordered Walesa's arrest. Nevertheless, demonstrations against government policies continued, and Walesa again became Solidarity's leader after his release in 1983. In addition, the labor movement found strong support among the clergy of the Roman Catholic Church. The head of the church, Pope John Paul II, was a Pole who was calling on Poland's Communist party to make reforms.

Recent Events

Walesa organized more protests in Gdansk in 1988. Facing mounting economic problems, the government agreed to legalize Solidarity and to end one-party rule. In June 1989, non-Communist candidates, many of them from Solidarity, won election to the legislature. The parliament then chose Jaruzelski as president and Tadeusz Mazowiecki as the prime minister. A Solidarity leader, Mazowiecki headed a coalition government that included Communist and non-Communist parties.

In January 1990, the leaders of the Polish Communist party renamed their organization Social Democracy of the Republic of Poland. Most Communist party property was turned over to the new government, which freed prices and wages and lifted all restrictions on the Polish media. The government also began selling state-owned companies to private investors—a process called privatization. As the nations of central and eastern Europe

turned away from Communism, Poland's newly privatized companies began doing business in western Europe.

After Walesa announced his candidacy for president in the fall of 1990, Jaruzelski resigned his office. The election then became a three-way race between Walesa, Mazowiecki, and Stanislaw Tyminski, a Polish-born businessman from Canada. When Walesa emerged as the victor in December 1990, Mazowiecki resigned his post as prime minister. Waldemar Pawlak, a leader of the Polish Peasants party, became prime minister in 1993.

During the early 1990s, the transition from a centrally planned economy to a free-market system caused severe problems, including falling production, high prices, and unemployment. Yet the government has been successful in attracting foreign investment and in selling off state-owned property. Poland's brisk trade with western European nations has helped the transition and has ended shortages of food and clothing. The benefits of democratic government and of an improving economy are allowing the Polish people to look forward to a better way of life.

Government

The 1989 agreement between the Communist government and the Solidarity union restructured the country's legislative bodies. Poland now has a bicameral (two-house) legislature known as the National Assembly. The Sejm, or lower house, consists of 460 locally elected representatives. The Senate, or upper house, has 100 members. The Sejm passes laws and approves government appointments. The Senate reviews—but cannot veto—legislation passed by the Sejm.

The president, who is elected by a popular vote to a five-year term, has broad powers, including the authority to conduct foreign policy and to oversee internal security. The president also may veto laws passed by the Sejm, which can then overturn the veto by a two-thirds vote. The president appoints the prime minister, who heads a council of ministers.

The Polish judicial system includes a supreme court, which makes final decisions on cases that come from the lower courts. A constitutional tribunal reviews legislation, and a state tribunal tries high-ranking government officials accused of breaking the law. Provincial courts hear criminal and civil cases, and local courts consider civil matters and minor crimes.

Poland consists of 49 provinces known as *voivodships*. Community councils govern the provinces as well as Poland's 830 towns and cities. An executive body oversees the operations of the council.

Before the vote of September 1993, nearly 30 political parties held seats in the Polish legislature. As a result of party rivalries, however, few laws were passed, and the chamber was often deadlocked. New laws passed in 1993 restricted seats in the legislature to parties winning at least 5 percent of the popular vote.

The driver of a horse-drawn carriage waits for passengers in Warsaw.

3) The People

From the time of the Piast dynasty until the 1950s, most Poles lived on farms. The few large cities that thrived from Poland's trade—such as Krakow, Warsaw, and Poznan—were home to a multiethnic population of Poles and other northern Europeans, including Germans, Dutch, and Scandinavians. Before World War II, Ukrainians, Czechs, and Belarussians also lived in Poland.

Rapid industrialization and the redrawing of Poland's borders after the war brought about great changes. The Soviet Union annexed a large part of eastern Poland, and most ethnic Germans fled to eastern Germany. New factories drew workers from the countryside, where state collectives forced many farmers off their land. By the early 1990s, ethnic Poles made up about 99 percent of Poland's population of 38.5 million, and more than 60 percent of the country's people were city dwellers.

A majority of Poles now live on the Central Plains, where Warsaw, Lodz, Poznan, and Wroclaw are located. Heavy industries and mines have made Silesia the country's most urbanized region. The Carpathian Forelands, with their fertile land and rich mineral resources, also are heavily populated.

Poland has one of the highest standards of living among the former European Communist countries. One of every 10 Poles has an automobile, and most families have both a radio and a television. Urban as well as rural Poles are suffering from a shortage of housing, however. Many of those seeking a new apartment must place their names on a long waiting list. The lack of housing forces many families to share crowded living quarters with their relatives.

Narrow houses line a public square in Gdansk. The center of Poland's shipbuilding industry, Gdansk was also the birthplace of Solidarity, which organized many rallies and strikes in the port during the 1980s.

Children offer goods for sale in Warsaw. During the 1980s, while state-owned businesses struggled to manufacture enough goods for Polish consumers, farmers and other producers openly sold plentiful merchandise on the streets.

Photo by George S. Thomson

The Church of the Virgin Mary towers above Market Square in Krakow. According to legend, the two brothers who built the church fell into a violent argument that ended in one brother's murder. Miraculously, the spire begun by the dead man grew taller than the one finished by his brother.

Religion

Since the Poles adopted Christianity in the tenth century, the Roman Catholic Church has had great influence in Poland. Loyalty to the Catholic church helped Poles keep their national identity during the era of partition and foreign rule in the 1800s. Later, when the Communist government restricted religious practices, some churches and seminaries remained open. Catholic leaders joined the opposition to the regime, and the Polish cardinal Karol Wojtyla, who became Pope John Paul II in 1978, used his power and popularity to press for reform.

Christmas and Easter are the major religious holidays in Poland. On Assumption Day, August 15, many Polish Catholics make a pilgrimage to the Jasna Gora Monastery at Czestochowa to honor the shrine of the Black Madonna. Devout Poles believe that this painting of the Virgin Mary stopped a Swedish invasion in the seventeenth century. The Black Madonna has since become an important symbol of the Polish nation.

More than 95 percent of Poles are Roman Catholic. The remainder are mostly Eastern Orthodox, Protestant, or Jewish. For centuries, Poland was an important center of Jewish religious, intellectual, and cultural life. The Jewish population was devastated by Nazi persecution during World War II, however, and most Jewish war survivors have emigrated from Poland.

Health and Education

The people of Poland generally enjoy good health. All workers and members of their

Courtesy of Sister Margaret Mewborter

Said to have supernatural powers, the Black Madonna of Czestochowa is a sacred relic of Poland's history. The two slashes in the cheek of the Virgin Mary were supposedly inflicted by an angry Tatar, who found the painting growing steadily heavier as he tried to steal it.

Photo by The Central Press—Foto Agency

A teacher instructs her class in a Polish elementary school. Poland's Communist government expanded education, yet the state also tightly controlled courses and textbooks. Since the fall of the Communist regime, several private schools have opened.

families—as well as pensioners, invalids, and students—receive free medical treatment at public clinics and hospitals. Group homes provide care for some retired workers and for people who are chronically ill or disabled.

Poland's heavy industrialization led to air and water pollution, especially in the industrial and mining cities of the south. As a result, health problems in the region include high rates of respiratory diseases and cancer. The average life expectancy is 71 years. The infant mortality rate in Poland is 14 per 1,000 live births. These are average figures among Poland's neighbors and among the former Communist nations of central Europe.

Poland's 79,000 physicians—one per 480 people—practice in 3,300 public, government-financed health centers. Since the end of Communist rule, there has been a growing private medical and dental practice available to those who can afford it.

Poles have always considered education important. Public education at all levels is free, and attendance is compulsory from ages 7 to 18. Poland's literacy rate—the percentage of adults who can read and write—has reached 98 percent. Until 1990 all Polish schools were operated by the state. Since then, numerous private schools have opened.

Elementary schools—which are in session five hours a day, five days a week—offer special classes and extracurricular activities after regular school hours. Athletic programs include soccer, bicycle racing, track and field, volleyball, and skiing.

After they have completed eighth grade, students may enroll in vocational schools or take an entrance exam for a secondary school of liberal arts. Students that pass this exam spend four years studying foreign languages, literature, art, music, and sciences.

Secondary-school graduates must pass entrance exams called *matura* before they can attend one of Poland's technical or general universities. Professional schools include medical schools, theological seminaries, and naval institutes. Specialty schools teach art, economics, and agriculture. Evening classes are available for adults, and special schools instruct disabled people as well as students who use languages other than Polish.

Languages and Literature

Polish is one of the West Slavic languages, a group that also includes Czech and Slovak. Widespread public education since World War II standardized written and spoken Polish, but regional dialects have survived. Silesian dialects, for example, are a mixture of Polish and German. The Gorale people of the Carpathian Mountains also have a distinctive dialect.

Poles take great pride in their literature, which has become an important expression of national identity. Poland's first literary works were lyric and epic poems that were sung or spoken. After the nation converted to Christianity, Latin became the dominant language for both secular and religious writing.

By the middle of the fifteenth century, Polish was replacing Latin as the nation's literary language. The sixteenth-century poet Jan Kochanowski wrote in both Latin and Polish. Mikolaj Rej (1505–1569) earned the title "The Father of Polish Literature" for satires, poems, and prose that he wrote exclusively in Polish. Later Polish writers produced important works of poetry, history, and religion.

Elaborate painting and calligraphy decorate an illuminated Polish book. Before the invention of movable type, books in Poland were written and bound by hand. Most of these works were religious texts in Latin, the universal language of the Roman Catholic Church.

After moving to Britain, Jozef Konrad Korzeniowski took the name Joseph Conrad. He mastered the English language and wrote popular adventure novels, many of which were based on his seafaring experiences.

Polish literature gained increasing importance during the 1800s. Poets such as Adam Mickiewicz kept Polish culture and patriotism alive during this period of partition and foreign rule. Mickiewicz's epic poem, *Lord Thaddeus,* expressed his deep love for Poland. Henryk Sienkiewicz received the Nobel Prize in literature in 1905 for his novel *Quo Vadis?*. The poet Czeslaw Milosz won the same prize in 1980.

Polish writers, many of whom became exiles, have made important contributions to other cultures. Jozef Konrad Korzeniowski moved to Britain, where he penned sea stories in English under the name Joseph Conrad. The works of Polish-

A modern building houses the Theater Muzyczny in Gdynia. Although Poland's Communist leaders restricted the work of writers and publishers, many of Poland's theater groups survived. Some even produced satirical plays that were openly critical of the regime.

Folk musicians perform for passersby in Warsaw.

born Isaac Bashevis Singer describe traditional Jewish myths and legends. Jerzy Kosinski, who like Singer emigrated to the United States, wrote *The Painted Bird*, a frightening account of the hardships experienced by Poles during World War II.

While in power, Poland's Communist regime placed heavy restrictions on authors and on the Polish media. Nevertheless, many Poles continued to publish their works underground. Poland now has one of the most active publishing industries in eastern Europe, with nearly 3,000 magazines and newspapers. Poles buy 200 million books a year, including popular novels that were not available during the Communist era.

Music, Drama, and Art

Poland's folk music has been renowned throughout Europe, and Polish classical composers stayed close to the nation's folk traditions. Many Polish composers of the nineteenth century wrote versions of the polonaise and the mazurka, Poland's national dances.

Poland's most famous composer, the pianist Frederic Chopin (1810–1849), left Poland to study and perform in France. He based much of his piano music—including polonaises, mazurkas, and waltzes—on Polish folk rhythms and melodies. Chopin's innovations in classical harmony made him a leading figure of nineteenth-century music.

Like Chopin, Ignace Jan Paderewski was a celebrated pianist who spent many years outside his homeland. A diplomat as well as a musician, Paderewski served as Poland's premier and foreign minister after World War I. Wanda Landowska, a Polish harpsichordist, was renowned for her performances of eighteenth-century music, especially the keyboard works of Johann Sebastian Bach.

45

Modern Poles enjoy many different musical styles, from classical to jazz to rock and roll. Western rock groups have toured in Polish cities, and jazz festivals take place each year in Wroclaw and Krakow. Karol Szymanowski and Krzysztof Penderecki have revolutionized concert music with their new approaches to musical harmony and structure.

Drama has been performed in Poland since the Piast dynasty. In the late 1700s, a Polish national theater was pioneered by the actor, director, and writer Wojciech Boguslawski. The nineteenth-century actress Helena Modrzejewska, who used the stage name Modjeska, performed Shakespearean plays and other dramas in Poland, western Europe, and the United States.

After World War II, Polish drama was used by the Communist government for political propaganda. The Popular Theater in Nowa Huta and the Dramatic Theater in Warsaw focused on moral and political problems. In the 1960s, student theaters combined the talents of painters, singers, actors, and jazz musicians to produce satirical comedy. These theaters provided a stage for writers whose printed works came under heavy censorhip by the Communist regime.

Like Polish musicians, Polish artists flourished during the 1800s. One of the most famous Polish painters, Jan Matejko of Krakow, produced historical scenes on huge canvases. His most famous painting is of Jan Sobieski's victory over the Turks at Vienna. Jozef Chelmonski, a well-known nineteenth-century realist, painted scenes from rural life.

Generations of rural families have kept Polish folk art alive. *Wycinanki*—paper cutouts made with scissors—originated in the 1800s. Common wycinanki designs depict trees, flowers, farm animals, and birds. Traditional folk art also includes rug and tapestry weaving, historic and religious woodcarving, pottery making, and painting on glass.

Sports

Poles enjoy a wide variety of recreational sports. The Carpathian Mountains in the

Aleksander Ford directed this scene from the movie *Krzyzacy* (also known as *Knights of the Teutonic Order*). Poland's film industry thrived after World War II, although many Polish directors, including Ford and Roman Polanski, left to work in other countries.

Gymnasts perform for a huge rally. Poland's Communist government encouraged amateur and school athletic clubs. In addition, the regime provided generous support to the country's Olympic athletes.

south offer miles of hiking trails, as well as rock climbing, camping, and skiing. The lakes of the north are favorite locations for sailing and waterskiing. Canoeists paddle the Czarna River in the Central Plains. A system of 17 national parks has been established in Poland's forests, mountains, and coastal areas.

Soccer, which Europeans call football, is Poland's most popular team sport. The nation takes pride in several outstanding professional soccer teams that draw spectators from across Europe. Basketball is played by amateur teams, and Polish volleyball squads have won gold medals in the Summer Olympic Games.

Soccer players duel in the stadium at Chorzow in southern Poland. The arena can hold more than 100,000 spectators.

Poles have set Olympic records in several sports. During the 1980 games, Wladyslaw Kozakiewicz broke the previous pole vault record, and Grazyna Rabsztyn set a new record in the 100-meter hurdles. Polish weightlifters and target shooters have also set new marks. Skiing celebrities include ski jumper Wojciech Fortuna and slalom skier Andrzej Bachleda.

Food

Polish meals vary according to what is available in each region. Along the Baltic coast, for example, herring is a staple food. Poles living in forested regions gather wild mushrooms and berries. Game—including boar, venison, and pheasant—is popular in the Carpathians. Traditional meals may also include locally grown potatoes, beets, cabbage, spinach, apples, pears, currants, or strawberries.

For centuries, Poles have eaten cabbage fresh or preserved it as sauerkraut. *Golabki* are cooked cabbage leaves stuffed with chopped meat and served with mushroom or tomato sauce. Other common foods are beetroot soup, *kielbasa* sausage, potatoes, sour cream, rye bread, and beer. Cooks stuff dough with meat, sauerkraut, fresh cabbage, potatoes, and cheese to make *pierogi. Bigos,* a popular stew that has many variations, combines meat, cabbage, sauerkraut, and seasonings. Favorite spices include dill, marjoram, and caraway seeds.

Many Poles begin the day with buttered bread and tea or coffee, sometimes accompanied by eggs, sausage, cheese, and ham or other sliced meats. Instead of lunch, Poles eat a second breakfast of bread and butter with cheese, sliced cucumbers, tomatoes, and tea. The late afternoon meal features soup, a meat or fish course, potatoes, vegetables, and a dessert of cakes or tarts. A late evening supper is often similar to breakfast.

Holiday meals are an occasion for festive gathering. During Christmas Eve, called *wigilia,* many Poles enjoy mushroom or fish soup, boiled carp, cabbage and mushrooms, noodles seasoned with poppy seeds, and stewed prunes. A typical Christmas dinner features ham, sausage, sauerkraut, and honey cakes called *pierniki.*

Diners enjoy a clear, sunny day from the tables of an outdoor restaurant.

Photo by The Central Press—Foto Agency

A woman adjusts spools of thread at a textile mill in Lodz. The city has been a center of cloth manufacturing since the nineteenth century.

4) The Economy

Before World War II, farming was Poland's most important economic activity. About two-thirds of the Polish people lived on farms, and the country was self-sufficient in food. During the late 1940s and 1950s, the Communist regime made a strong effort to industrialize the country. The government built new plants to produce steel, chemicals, and textiles and encouraged farmers to seek factory jobs in Polish cities.

With the rural population declining, however, half as many farmers were expected to feed Poland's growing urban population. Shortages of food and other items worsened, and living standards fell. Poland had to borrow heavily to keep its industries running and to import needed goods. Strikes and demonstrations during the 1980s eventually ended Polish Communism and led to the establishment of a free-market economy.

After the fall of the Communist regime, the new government began privatizing—selling its state-owned businesses to private investors. Poland ended much of its central planning and lifted controls on prices and wages. No longer owned or supported by the state, inefficient firms cut back their operations or went out of business. The result has been rising unemployment.

Although the cost of food and consumer goods has increased sharply, privatization is forcing many firms to become more productive in order to survive. The country has delayed payments on its heavy foreign debt and is gaining development aid from western Europe and the United States. A weak domestic market, however, prevents the growth of many companies, and foreign trade has become the key to a successful Polish economy.

Manufacturing and Trade

As Poland's industries expanded, the country began making new products, including electronic equipment, ships, agricultural fertilizers, and chemicals. Manufacturing became Poland's major economic activity, employing about 25 percent of the workforce and producing half of the nation's goods and services. The Polish government maintains control over heavy industries, such as steel production, but smaller firms and manufacturing plants are being privatized.

Poland's chief industrial area is Silesia, a region of heavy manufacturing, mining, and energy production in the southwest. Factories in Warsaw and Krakow make steel, textiles, electronic equipment, and building materials. Gdansk and Gdynia, key Baltic Sea ports, boast large shipbuilding industries. For more than a

A construction crew prepares for the opening of a new manufacturing facility. This joint venture will employ Polish workers to assemble clothing for a foreign company.

Photo by George S. Thomson

Cranes loom over Gdynia's harbor, an important center of shipping and cargo handling on the Baltic coast.

century, the textile mills at Lodz produced woolen and cotton products for export to Russia. Other major Polish industries manufacture cement, appliances, agricultural fertilizers, and processed foods.

During the 1980s, Poland traded mainly with other Communist nations and with developing countries in Asia, Africa, and the Middle East. Poland's industrialization made it a leading exporter of raw materials and building supplies to these regions. As many Communist countries changed their economic systems in the early 1990s, the Soviet-led trading bloc in eastern Europe fell apart, and Poland's trade with western nations increased.

The country now has a trade surplus, meaning it sells more goods than it buys. This surplus allows Poland to invest in new manufacturing plants and equipment. To promote Polish goods abroad, the government has signed treaties with the United States and with the European Community (EC), an association of western European

Independent Picture Service

Many high-rises, including these apartments near Wroclaw, were raised in the suburbs of Polish cities after World War II. The buildings housed workers who were arriving in urban areas to labor in nearby factories and mills.

This plant in Bielawa produces cement, an important construction material. Built under Poland's Communist regime, the huge plant is struggling to survive tough trade competition and a weak economy.

Farmers harvest grain from a plowed field. With the introduction of machinery on state-owned farms, Poland's crop yields increased. Yet the most productive lands under the Communist regime were privately owned.

nations that have formed a common trading market.

Minerals, finished metals, and raw materials—such as coal, copper, and sulfur—are important Polish exports. Poland imports machinery, food, crude oil, cotton, and iron ore. The leading sources of imported goods are Germany, the Czech Republic, Slovakia, Belarus, and Ukraine.

Agriculture, Forestry, and Fishing

After World War II, Poland's government organized many private farms into state-owned collective farms. Farmers on the collectives shared their labor and equipment. The government paid a fixed wage and required the collectives to sell all of their produce to the state. By the 1950s, nearly half of Poland's land had been collectivized.

At the end of the 1950s, however, the collective-farm system was failing. Hired farmers did not take proper care of agricultural machinery. Because they earned fixed wages, they had little incentive to produce a bigger harvest. To profit in an underground market for food, some farmers underreported their harvests and kept produce to sell privately.

The food shortages that resulted from these practices led the government to return Polish farms to private ownership, although the state still controlled the use of fertilizers and machinery. By the early 1990s, more than two million family farms existed in Poland. Because the costs of fertilizers, pesticides, and energy are high, many of these farmers do not use chemicals or modern machinery to cultivate their crops.

Independent Picture Service

Farmers use a pair of tractors to cultivate and seed a rural field. The government provided state-run farming collectives with fertilizers, seed, and machinery.

Photo by The Central Press—Foto Agency

Workers use nets to collect amber from the shores of the Baltic Sea. Made from the fossilized resin of ancient trees, amber is often combined with silver to create expensive jewelry.

A sawmill laborer wrestles a heavy log into position. Timber cutting remains an important economic activity in Poland, where demand is high for lumber as well as for paper products. Mining operations also buy heavy logs to use as overhead supports in underground shafts.

Photo © John R. Kreul

Poland's most important crops are grains such as wheat, rye, oats, and barley, which are processed for livestock feed, for domestic food markets, or for alcoholic beverages. Rapeseed, a forage crop for sheep and pigs, is also made into a useful oil. The vast Central Plains, the fertile Polish Uplands, and the Carpathian Forelands produce most of Poland's grain. These regions also yield vegetable crops, including potatoes and sugar beets. The raising of livestock, especially cattle and sheep, is important in southern Poland.

About 25 percent of Poland is covered by forests, mostly pine, spruce, and other evergreens. Sawmills in the Lake Region and in the Carpathian Mountains cut about 19 million tons of wood every year for pulp to make paper and paper products. Mills also process lumber for use in new construction and for mine-shaft supports.

Poland's commercial fishing companies catch 65,000 tons of fish annually. Small fishing ports, including Darlowo and Ustka, line the Baltic coast, processing herring and cod from the Baltic and North seas and from the open waters of the North Atlantic Ocean.

Mining and Energy

Coal is Poland's most important mineral resource. The extensive deposits in Silesia have made this region one of the world's leading exporters of coal. Fields in southern and southwestern Poland hold an estimated 86 billion tons of both bituminous (hard) coal and lignite (soft) coal—a supply that will last 600 years at the current rate of production. The largest field lies near Katowice, a major mining and metal-processing center.

The Polish Uplands contain reserves of copper, zinc, lead, and sulfur. Although Polish companies mine small amounts of iron ore, the country must import additional iron for its large steel and ship-building industries.

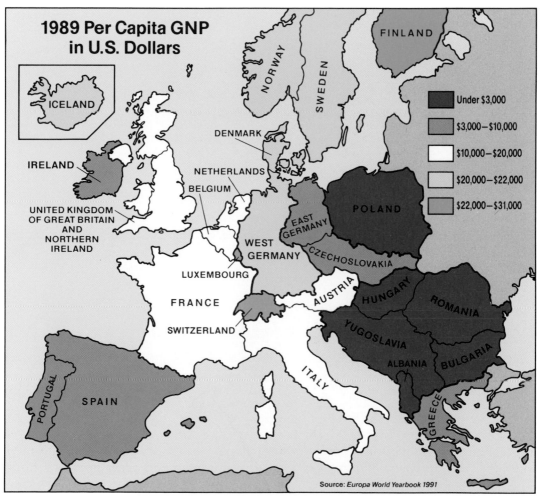

1989 Per Capita GNP in U.S. Dollars

Legend:
- Under $3,000
- $3,000–$10,000
- $10,000–$20,000
- $20,000–$22,000
- $22,000–$31,000

Source: *Europa World Yearbook 1991*

Artwork by Laura Westlund

This chart compares the average productivity per person—calculated by gross national product (GNP) per capita—for 26 European countries in 1989. The GNP is the value of all goods and services produced by a country in a year. To arrive at the GNP per capita, each nation's total GNP is divided by its population. The Polish figure of $1,760 made the country one of Europe's least productive, yet Poland avoided the sharp economic decline that has hit other former Communist nations, many of which are experiencing sharp drops in their GNP figures. In the early 1990s, Poland's per-capita GNP rose to nearly $1,900.

Photo by The Central Press—Foto Agency

Poland still has a few operating oil wells, but production is too low to meet demand. The country must import most of its crude oil.

A rich supply of rock salt exists in southern and central Poland. The salt mine at Wieliczka, near Krakow, has produced salt for many centuries. Amber, a semi-precious stone formed from fossilized tree resin, exists in small deposits along the coast of the Baltic Sea. Workshops polish the material and shape it into jewelry.

The oil fields of Poland stretch across 9,000 square miles in the foothills of the Carpathian Mountains. The supply of domestic crude oil, however, cannot meet

Independent Picture Service

A gigantic crane digs mineral ore from a hillside at a mine near Nowa Huta. The surrounding region of Silesia has one of the world's largest deposits of coal, most of which is used to fuel plants that generate electricity.

the demand created by the country's factories, homes, and motor vehicles. As a result, Poland must import 95 percent of its oil. Power plants that burn hard coal and lignite generate most of the nation's electricity. Hydroelectric plants on the Vistula River and along other waterways supply additional power.

Tourism

Every year, more than 18 million people visit Poland, bringing more than $1 billion in foreign currency into the Polish economy. Although Poland lacks the warm and sunny climate favored by many European travelers, the country boasts historical and cultural treasures, as well as recreational spots and health resorts.

In Krakow tourists may explore the Wawel Cathedral and an impressive historical museum in Wawel Castle.

Independent Picture Service

The huge petrochemical factory at Plock employs thousands of workers to make a wide variety of industrial goods.

Independent Picture Service

Sailboats catch the prevailing breezes on one of the Masurian Lakes in northeastern Poland. This region is a favorite spot for summer vacationers.

Niedzica Castle looms over the rolling hills of southern Poland. More than 450 Polish castles, many of which remain open as historical museums, have survived wars and invasions.

Visitors to the Wieliczka salt mine tour worked-out chambers and view salt statues and chandeliers in the Chapel of the Blessed King. The Castle of the Teutonic Knights at Malbork, near Gdansk, is an impressive ancient stronghold. The Amber Museum in the castle displays prehistoric plants and insects preserved in ancient amber resin.

Many of Poland's popular sites date to World War II. A museum at the site of the Auschwitz concentration camp, west of Krakow, reminds visitors of the millions who were killed there by the Nazis. Tourists in Warsaw's Castle Square visit the rebuilt statue of King Sigismund III Vasa, who made Warsaw the Polish capital. The pieces of the original statue, shattered during World War II, are on display nearby.

Photo © John R. Kreul

Tourists gather at a historic bridge that crosses the Vistula River in the center of Warsaw.

Courtesy of Polish National Tourist Office

The Sukiennice (Cloth Hall) in Krakow's Market Square dates to the 1500s. Once a busy textile exchange, the Sukiennice now holds a gallery of eighteenth- and nineteenth-century Polish paintings. In front of the building stands a statue of Adam Mickiewicz, Poland's most renowned poet.

Ferries dock at the busy waterfront in Gdansk. A ferry service links the city to Britain, Denmark, and Sweden, as well as to other Polish Baltic ports.

Skiing resorts, such as Zakopane in the Tatra Mountains, draw winter vacationers. The Vistula and other rivers attract canoeists, and the Baltic coast is famous for its mineral-water spas. Poland's horse-breeding establishments give tourists an opportunity to enjoy riding tours through the countryside, where many old manor houses and palaces are open for overnight stays. Visitors can also take pleasant horse-drawn carriage rides through the Bialowieza Forest.

Transportation

Poland's extensive transportation network includes road, rail, air, and inland shipping systems. Although this network links nearly all of the country's cities and regions, much of the equipment used is obsolete. Repair and improvements are especially needed on Poland's roads and highways.

Poland's railroads, which were developed in the years before World War I, are the most reliable and common means of ship-

Icebreakers clear dangerous floating ice from a section of the Odra River. An important shipping route within Poland, the Odra is often closed to traffic during the winter.

Poland's national airline, LOT, serves many international destinations. This plane, however, flies mostly shorter routes within the country.

ping goods on land. The system was most advanced in the western and central regions, which were under German administration in the late 1800s. Much of the rail network, however, was destroyed during World War II. The government converted main lines to electric power in the postwar years. For the next four decades, the rail system transported freight between neighboring countries and Polish ports.

Poland's railroads now run on 16,500 miles of track, about a quarter of which is electrified. Railroads link cities, ports, and many of the larger towns. Diesel and electric express trains carry most passengers, while steam engines move long-distance freight.

Poland's 190,000 miles of roads include several important trans-European routes. Since the early 1970s, the highway system has expanded and improved as the number of cars, trucks, and buses has increased. Modern routes exist throughout the nation, but the network of freeways is limited. Although half of the roads are paved, main roads are often in poor condition. Cars and horse-drawn carts must share the narrow local streets, many of which are unpaved.

The country's rivers and seacoast have been important for transportation and trade since early times. A system of canals connects waterways and inland ports, including Warsaw and Wroclaw. Barges and small freighters ply the Vistula and Odra rivers. Ships carry coal to the port of Szczecin along the Odra, which is linked by the Gliwice Canal to the industrial and mining centers of Silesia. International shipping moves through the Baltic ports of Gdansk, Gdynia, and Szczecin.

LOT, the national airline, has both international and domestic flights. It serves Warsaw—the site of Poland's largest international airport—and five other Polish cities.

Students gather in the courtyard of the Catholic University of Lublin, the only religious college allowed to operate in Communist Europe. Since the 1980s, the Polish government has dropped restrictions on subjects taught at public universities.

A narrow railway passes through the mountains of southern Poland.

The Future

The 1990s have brought many changes for Poles as the government has introduced extensive economic reforms. Although these measures have caused high prices and rising unemployment, most Poles support the establishment of a market economy. By late 1993 the state had privatized most of the country's smaller firms, and private companies were employing more than half of all Polish workers.

The market reforms have also caused turmoil, however, as Poland's leaders and political parties clash over the country's economic future. Many politicians favor increased spending for unemployment benefits and social programs. Other officials seek to reduce spending to balance the national budget and to attract new loans and investment. Trade unions, which sparked the anti-Communist strikes of the 1980s, are pressuring the new government with demands for better wages and working conditions.

The pollution of Poland's air and water is another major problem. While western European countries were taking measures to control industrial pollution, the Communist governments of central and eastern Europe sought only to increase production. Environmental dangers were not considered, and many Polish cities are suffering the consequences. Dirty air and polluted underground water are slowly destroying many of the country's buildings and historic monuments. In addition, heavily industrialized cities are suffering high rates of cancer and other diseases.

Poles have survived hard times in the past and are hopeful about their future. Throughout a turbulent history, they kept their national identity even when overrun and ruled by foreign nations. Poland has become an economic leader among the former Communist nations of eastern Europe, and the Polish people are eagerly taking advantage of their new opportunities.

A shiny sedan idles outside a modern villa. Many members of Poland's middle class have built new vacation homes in the countryside.

Index